Sound Trackers

1980s Pop

SOUND TRACKERS – 1980s POP
was produced by

David West Children's Books
5-11 Mortimer Street
London W1N 7RH

Picture research: Brooks Krikler Research
Editor: Clare Oliver

First published in Great Britain in 1998 by
Heinemann Library, Halley Court, Jordan Hill, Oxford OX2 8EJ, a division of
Reed Educational and Professional Publishing Limited.

OXFORD MELBOURNE AUCKLAND
JOHANNESBURG BLANTYRE GABORONE
IBADAN PORTSMOUTH (NH) USA CHICAGO

01 00 99 98
10 9 8 7 6 5 4 3 2 1

ISBN 0 431 09094 7 (HB)
ISBN 0 431 09098 X (PB)

British Library Cataloguing in Publication Data

Brunning, Bob
1980s pop. – (Sound trackers)
1. Popular music – 1981 - 1990 – Juvenile literature
I. Title II .Nineteen eighties' pop
781. 6 ' 4 ' 09048

Printed and bound in Italy.

1980s Pop

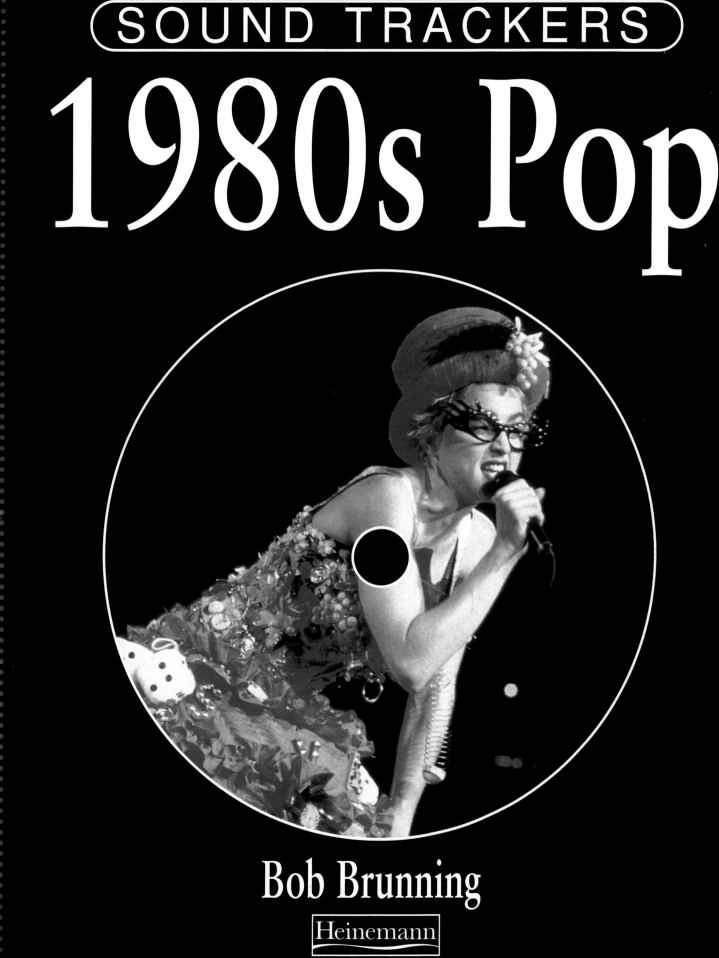

Bob Brunning

Heinemann

CONTENTS

20235

T80·42

On these discs is a selection of the artists' recordings. Many of these albums are now available on CD. If they are not, many of the tracks from them can be found on compilation CDs.

Elton John

These boxes give you extra information about the artists and their times.

Some contain anecdotes about the artists themselves or about the people who helped their careers or, occasionally, about those who exploited them.

Others provide historical facts about the music, lifestyles, fans and fashions of the day.

INTRODUCTION

The 1980s were a turbulent time. High unemployment and worldwide political instability caused many problems.

The author Bob Brunning talks to Mark Knopfler at the famous 100 Club in London.

The music business experienced changes, too. Ex-Beatle John Lennon was murdered outside his New York apartment in 1980 and reggae's undisputed king, Bob Marley, succumbed to cancer in '81. Other sad losses included blues singer Muddy Waters, Bill Haley, Karen Carpenter, Beach Boy Dennis Wilson and Marvin Gaye.

The baby-boomers grew up, but did not grow away from music: there was a wave of stadium rockers to suit this older audience. And Bob Geldof invented 'charity rock' when he organised the biggest pop event in history – Live Aid.

Meanwhile, technology marched on. Synthesisers heralded the age of electronic music. State-of-the-art production could finally be appreciated with the advent of the CD. (Critics confidently predicted that the format would never be popular!) As the '80s drew to a close, revolutionary styles were emerging. Rap stripped down songs until they were punchy, spoken poems; techno stripped away all but the barest repetitive beats.

The fact that it is so difficult to pinpoint one particular sound for the decade only goes to show what a creative, exciting decade for pop it was.

DIRE STRAITS

Few guitarists can be identified after listening to just a few bars of their playing, but Mark Knopfler is one of them. His lyrical, blues-based style brought huge success for his band, Dire Straits. But this did not happen overnight. Knopfler discovered his love of music a little later than some performers.

A LATE START

Mark had already pursued careers as a journalist and a teacher when, aged 28, he left Newcastle and headed to London with his younger brother David. David's flatmate, John Illsley, also took the plunge and joined Dire Straits alongside the experienced session drummer Pick Withers. The band couldn't have timed their entry into London's pub rock scene more badly. Punk reigned, and the delicate music of the Straits could hardly compete with all that fury and angst.

CD KINGS

Launched in the early 1980s, the compact disc (CD) promised – and delivered – top quality reproduction and it didn't scratch like an LP.

It appealed to 'yuppies' (young urban professionals) with money to spend. At the same time the baby-boomers – who'd started buying pop music as teenagers in the '60s – had grown up. Suddenly there was a much bigger audience for AOR (Adult-Oriented Rock). Dire Straits' easy rock was ideal for this new, mature market. 'Brothers In Arms' was the first album to go platinum on CD alone.

NOT-SO-DIRE STRAITS

Mark returned to teaching, but did not give up on Dire Straits. In 1978 the band released the classic 'Sultans Of Swing'. It was a worldwide hit. In June, the band released their debut album, 'Dire Straits' – which went gold! It made the UK and US Top 10s, and so did their second album, 'Communiqué'.

MAKING MOVES

David Knopfler left the band, wishing to pursue a solo career, and so the band's line-up changed.

'Dire Straits'
June '78
'Communiqué'
August '79
'Making Movies'
October '80
'Love Over Gold'
September '82

'Alchemy: Dire Straits Live'
March '84
'Brothers In Arms'
May '85
'Money For Nothing'
October '88

The next album, 'Making Movies', marked a shift in musical direction. The sound was jazzier, the production tighter and the style more lyrical; for example, 'Romeo And Juliet' retold the classic tragedy in a modern setting.

Knopfler 'scored' films including 'Cal' (above) in 1984.

STRENGTH TO STRENGTH

The atmospheric album 'Love Over Gold' followed in 1982, then the Straits took to the road. The result was a fine live double album, 'Alchemy'. Next came their biggest album success to date: 'Brothers In Arms' sold nine million copies! Knopfler gave a working man's view of rock superstardom with the witty 'Money For Nothing', and three other singles from the album were hits.

CLASS ACT

Knopfler pursued other projects in the late 1980s, but in '91 Dire Straits released a new album and went on tour. And as fans continue to lap up his superb guitar playing and songwriting, it is unlikely that we will see Mark Knopfler back in the front of the class!

In 1989 Mark Knopfler formed the fun country band the Notting Hillbillies. Their album, 'Missing... Presumed Having A Good Time' reached No. 2 in the UK charts.

The EURYTHMICS

The career of Dave Stewart and Annie Lennox's successful band, the Eurythmics spans the decade. Their first hit came in 1979, and the two finally split up in '90. Guitarist Stewart and singer Lennox met in London in 1976 and fell head over heels in love. (Dave's first words to her were "Will you marry me?"). Together with guitarist Pete Coombes, they formed a band called Catch, but soon renamed themselves the Tourists.

STRICTLY FOR THE TOURISTS

Joined by bassist Eddy Chin and drummer Jim Toomey, the Tourists recorded their debut album in 1979. The same year, they had minor hits with their single, 'The Loneliest Man In The World', and a second album, 'Reality Effect'. And their next two singles both made the Top 10. The best was yet to come. In late 1980, the Tourists disbanded, and Stewart and Lennox formed the Eurythmics.

The Tourists were a hit in London's post-punk pubs and clubs.

SWEET DREAMS ARE MADE OF THIS...

By now, their romance was over, but the couple's working relationship was as strong as ever. The Eurythmics' first five singles flopped, but in January 1983 they released 'Sweet Dreams (Are Made Of This)'. The single topped the charts on both sides of the Atlantic, and the album of the same name – with its robotic, synthesiser sound – was a great success. In July the same year, the Eurythmics released the haunting 'Who's That Girl?', another smash hit taken from their new chart-topping album, 'Touch'. The hits kept coming: from the up-tempo, and very catchy, 'Right By Your Side' to the maudlin 'Here Comes The Rain Again' which finally took the Eurythmics into the US Top 5.

Aware of the importance of image, Stewart chose his costumes with care.

SHOWING OFF

People flocked to their concerts, thrilled by the startling special effects and the snappy image presented by Lennox. During the 1984 Grammy Awards ceremony, Lennox flaunted her gender-bending image by performing in drag!

SOUL-SEARCHING

More hits followed. Between May 1985 and June '90, four of the Eurythmics' albums and 13 of their singles entered the Top 40. The duo moved away from 'synth-pop' towards rhythm and blues (R&B). For a track on their fourth album 'Be Yourself Tonight', they worked with the legendary singer Aretha Franklin on 'Sisters Are Doin' It For Themselves'. In 1988 Lennox contributed to soul giant Al Green's, 'Put A Little Love In Your Heart'. At the end of the '80s, the talented pair went their separate ways. Both have gone on to enjoy tremendous – and well-deserved – success in their solo careers.

'Sweet Dreams (Are Made Of This)'
January '83
'Touch'
November '83
'Be Yourself Tonight'
May '85

'Revenge'
July '86
'Savage'
November '87
'We Too Are One'
September '89
'Greatest Hits'
May '91

GOING SOLO

Annie Lennox and Dave Stewart wasted no time in establishing themselves as solo performers. Lennox released her sublime single 'Why' in March 1992. In the same year her album 'Diva' made the No. 1 spot, and provided two more hit singles. In 1995 her covers album 'Medusa' also topped the charts and led to a hit with her version of 'A Whiter Shade Of Pale'. Dave Stewart has written soundtracks and recorded several solo albums, including the excellent 'Greetings From The Gutter'. He is also a very successful producer: his credits include work with such stars as Mick Jagger, Bob Geldof, Bob Dylan and Tom Petty.

MICHAEL JACKSON

Michael Joseph Jackson was born on the 29 August 1958 in Gary, Indiana. At an age when most youngsters would be nervously starting primary school, five-year-old Jackson joined four of his eight brothers and sisters on the road in the Jackson 5. Already a talented singer, dancer and immensely confident performer, his contribution to the group rapidly outstripped the novelty value of his extreme youth.

AN EXTRAORDINARY CHILDHOOD

The Motown record company spotted the potential of the all-singing, all-dancing quintet, and signed them – when Michael was just ten years old. The boys had four No. 1s in 1970 and their first two albums entered the Top 10. In 1972, Motown brought out Michael's first solo single 'Got To Be There' and for almost a decade Michael juggled two careers; one as a successful solo singer, and the other as a member of the Jackson 5.

THE 1970s

In 1976, Michael appeared in his first movie, a musical called 'The Wiz'.

Young Michael fronts the Jackson 5.

He worked on the soundtrack with producer, Quincy Jones. In 1979 Jackson and Jones produced the soul album 'Off The Wall'. It sold over seven million copies and stayed in the charts for five years. Jackson won a Grammy award for the first single from the album, 'Don't Stop 'Til You Get Enough', which was a No. 1 in the USA and UK.

A Michael Jackson doll.

'Forever, Michael'
March '75
'Off The Wall'
August '79
'Thriller'
December '82
'Michael Jackson Anthology'
April '87

'Bad'
September '87
'Dangerous'
December '91
'HIStory Past, Present & Future, Book 1'
June '95

THRILLING SUCCESS

In 1982, Jackson released 'Thriller', which eventually became the best-selling album of all time. It sold 42 million copies, stayed at No. 1 in the USA for 21 weeks, and provided seven Top 10 singles. 'Thriller' was nominated for a record-breaking twelve Grammys; in the event, Jackson and Jones won eight of the awards.

Topping 'Thriller' would challenge any performer, and Jackson couldn't quite manage it. However, 'Bad' sold three million copies in two months, and the first four singles lifted from it made No. 1. By anybody else's standards, it was an enormous hit! By now the most famous man in the world, 'Jacko' gave sell-out tours, dazzling audiences with his spectacular dancing prowess.

DARKER DAYS

From the early 1980s, Jackson had been portrayed in the media as an eccentric 'Peter Pan' figure – the boy who refused to grow up. He had a funfair built in his own garden and seemed more at home with children and animals than other adults. As the decade drew to a close, his personal life attracted more and more attention: the tabloids reported on his extensive plastic surgery and his ever-paler skin. In the 1990s, unproven allegations of child abuse severely damaged Jackson's reputation, and his short-lived marriage to Lisa Marie Presley (daughter of Elvis) did little to remedy this. Still, nothing can detract from his phenomenal contribution to pop music.

MTV NATION

The first-ever television channel aimed solely at music-lovers was launched in the USA in 1981 and in Europe six years later.

MTV broadcast music videos around the clock and before long, the 'promo' was crucial to a record's success. 'Thriller' expertly made use of the new medium: every single from the album was promoted with a stunning video. The hype for MTV's unveiling of the 'Thriller' video was enormous – and well-deserved. More like a mini movie, it starred Michael Jackson in a frightening fantasy world against a backdrop of stunning effects.

Michael Jackson and ghouls pose for a promotional shot for the amazing 'Thriller' video.

ELTON JOHN

Reginald Kenneth Dwight was born on 25 March 1947 in Pinner, Middlesex. At four, he started piano lessons and this early promise certainly didn't fade. By the age of 11, Reginald was studying at London's prestigious Royal Academy of Music. However, Reg was turning on to the pop music of the day: rock 'n' roll and rhythm and blues. He abandoned the classics and hit the road with rhythm and blues band Bluesology in 1961.

A FAIRYTALE PARTNERSHIP

However, in 1966, singer Long John Baldry joined the band, pushing Dwight out. He responded to an ad placed by Liberty Records, who put him in touch with another aspiring writer. Neither knew it at the time, but the pair eventually became one of the most successful songwriting partnerships of all time.

Reg Dwight was now Elton John, and his new partner was 17-year-old Bernie Taupin. A pattern was quickly established: Elton wrote the music, Taupin, the lyrics and they communicated by post and phone. They wrote 20 songs together before they even met! It was a winning formula. In August 1970, 'Your Song' entered the USA charts, albeit at a lowly 92. His first album, 'Elton John', featured his new band – Caleb Quaye (guitar), Dee Murray (bass) and Nigel Olsson (drums). It went to No. 4 in the USA and entered the UK Top 10.

John, Olsson and Murray in 1970.

'Elton John'
April '70
'Tumbleweed Connection'
October '70
'Honky Chateau'
May '72
'Goodbye Yellow Brick Road'
October '73

'Too Low For Zero'
May '83
'Breaking Hearts'
July '84
'Sleeping With The Past'
August '89

GLAMOROUS ROCKER

Elton John's mesmerising, larger-than-life stage persona and Taupin's catchy lyrics ensured dozens of hits throughout the 1970s, such as 'Rocket Man', 'Daniel' and 'Don't Go Breakin' My Heart' (with Kiki Dee).

THE MIDAS TOUCH

Towards the end of the 1970s Elton's career slowed down. He had serious problems with alcohol and drug abuse, and briefly fell out with Taupin. But with the release of 'Too Low For Zero' ('83), the pair had another run of hits. The album went gold and featured several hit singles, including the defiant 'I'm Still Standing', and melodic 'I Guess That's Why They Call It The Blues'.

Elton starred in the cult movie, 'Tommy' released in 1975.

For the rest of the decade every album he released earned a gold disc. By 1988, he had reached a turning point. He overcame his drug addiction at last. And a new, mature Elton announced that all future royalties from his singles would go towards AIDS research.

STILL BURNING BRIGHT

For the funeral of Princess Diana in 1997, Elton John rearranged his haunting anthem, 'Candle in the Wind', as a tribute to her. His moving performance reduced millions of viewers to tears. In 1998, Reg Dwight became Sir Elton John – a just recognition for one of the most successful pop stars of all time.

A MATCH MADE IN HEAVEN

While Elton worked on the tunes, ace lyricist Bernie Taupin wrote the words. Taupin respected Elton's skills and didn't begrudge him the limelight. Follow the notes below and see if you can identify this Taupin/John classic.

Bernie Taupin made a rare public appearance at a book-signing session with Elton John.

MADONNA

Madonna Louise Veronica Ciccone was born in Rochester, Michigan on 16 August 1959. One of seven children, she quickly learnt to use her natural talents as a singer, dancer, actress, pianist and all round show-off to get attention. Her ballet skills won her a scholarship to the University of Michigan, but she didn't stay long. Madonna was already beginning to demonstrate her restlessness and, more importantly, her ability to recognise – and seize – a good opportunity when she saw one.

BIG DEAL

After several false starts, Madonna finally signed with Sire Records in 1982. Sire, a subsidiary of entertainment giants, Warner Brothers, had faith in Madonna, and were prepared to spend money promoting her – it paid off! The singer achieved a few minor club hits before her debut album, 'Madonna', hit the US and UK Top 10s in 1983. Many of the songs were written in collaboration with her ex-boyfriend Steve Bray and they were all slickly produced. Her pop hit, 'Holiday', made the Top 40, but with the catchy 'Lucky Star', Madonna scaled to No. 4 in the charts.

TEEN IDOL

Madonna cultivated and revelled in her extravagant image and, of course, showed off her real talent as both a singer and dancer.

In July 1985, Madonna performed at Live Aid USA.

ACTING AMBITION

Madonna was already a pop success when she starred with Rosanna Arquette in the box office blockbuster, 'Desperately Seeking Susan' ('85). But she floundered with her next two films – 'Shanghai Surprise' ('86), alongside her (now ex-) husband Sean Penn, and 'Who's That Girl' ('87). She received good reviews for her work opposite Warren Beatty in her next film, 'Dick Tracy' ('90) about the comic strip sleuth. 'A League Of Their Own' ('92) was nothing special – a run-of-the-mill baseball film. But at last, in 1996, Madonna secured a part she'd been after for eight years. It was worth the wait. She won a Golden Globe for her mature performance in the film musical 'Evita', as Argentinian first lady, Eva Perón. Madonna the actress had finally made it!

Madonna's 'Evita' won the Golden Globe for Best Actress.

Her next album, 'Like A Virgin', was a No. 1 in the UK and USA. Supported by the first of many raunchy videos, it was followed by no less than ten more hits. She had universal appeal but was especially popular in the teen market: young boys swooned over her upfront sexiness, while girls admired her raw ambition – and her wild, eccentric taste in clothes!

MATERIAL GIRL

Ten chart hits followed, each selling millions of copies. Naked ambition was the theme for 'Material Girl', in which she re-invented herself as a Marilyn Monroe-style femme fatale. 'Crazy For You' proved she was just as at home with soulful ballads and 'Vogue' cashed in on the very latest – and very short-lived – spiky dance craze, the Vogue.

IN THE PUBLIC EYE

Madonna had achieved her ambition of becoming an international superstar, as an actress as well as a singer, but with this came tabloid attention. Her tempestous relationships with a string of larger-than-life partners kept the press busy. So did the publication of her controversial photo album, 'Sex', which featured erotic photos of Madonna – and friends. The first print run sold out within days, and the coffee-table book reprinted several times.

TODAY

Today Madonna has left her raunchy image behind, but shows no signs of slowing down – on the movie *or* music fronts.

Madonna and daughter Lourdes Maria Ciccone Leon, who was born in 1996.

The POLICE

In the northern English town of Newcastle, Gordon Sumner, a schoolteacher, was enjoying working with his jazz group, Last Exit. He was dismissive of rock and pop music but two musicians who attended one of his gigs had other ideas. Stewart Copeland and Henry Padovani wanted to form a rock band. The pair persuaded Sumner, nicknamed 'Sting', to join them and the Police were born. It was 1977.

AWAITING FAME

They immediately adopted their characteristic spare, slightly punky and definitely reggae-based style. Copeland made a feature of his unusual drum style (his kit was set up the wrong way round). On the brink of fame, the Police were hard up and agreed to appear on a chewing gum ad. They happily dyed their hair blonde for the ad – and kept the look for a while.

RECORDING SUCCESS

In April 1978 the Police made the first of many brilliant records. 'Roxanne' was not an instant hit but later in '78 they released 'Can't Stand Losing You'. Padovani left, unwilling to play second fiddle to Sting and in came Andy Summers.

'Outlandos d'Amour'
October '78
'Regatta de Blanc'
October '79
'Zenyatta Mondatta'
October '80

'Synchronicity'
June '83
'Every Breath You Take: The Singles'
November '86

Gordon Sumner (Sting)

Stewart Copeland (drums)

The first album, 'Outlandos d'Amour' was released in late 1978 and contained a challenging collection of songs. 'Roxanne', their song about a young man's love for a prostitute, had reggae-styled verses and a rocking harmony chorus. It was re-released in '79 and finally made it into the charts, despite a BBC ban in the UK.

MAGIC!

In the 1980s, the Police made it big, starting with their claustrophobic single 'Don't Stand So Close to Me'. Perfect, catchy pop seemed to come naturally to the Police. 'Every Little Thing She Does Is Magic' taken from the album 'Ghost In The Machine' was another sing-along tune. Sting's voice always seemed strained with emotion, but never more so than on the creepy classic, 'Every Breath You Take'. The single appeared on 'Synchronicity', the melancholic but humorous album which marked the peak of their career. The Police have not recorded any new material together since.

SAVE THE RAINFORESTS

Environmental issues came to the fore during the '80s. In particular, there was concern that large areas of tropical rainforest were being cleared for timber at the expense of countless species of plants and animals. The forests were also home to tribal Indians who had lived there for centuries.

Sting had taken part in Amnesty International's 'Human Rights Now!' tour, which took him all over the world. What he saw in South America led him to campaign about the Indians in the Brazilian rainforest whose homelands were being sold off to loggers by the Brazilian government.

With Chief Raoni, Sting pleads for rainforest conservation.

SLEEPING PARTNERS

Oddly, although they ceased performing in the mid-'80s, the Police never officially 'broke up', and none of them has shut the door on the idea of the band re-forming. But don't hold your breath! Today Sting, Summers and Copeland all enjoy successful solo careers. 'Dream Of The Blue Turtles' ('85) was Sting's first solo album and illustrated his strong jazz influences. He has also performed some accomplished acting roles in movies such as 'Quadrophenia', 'Radio On', 'Brimstone And Treacle' and 'Dune'.

How on Earth did Sting also find time for his sterling work in campaigning to conserve the Brazilian rainforests?

Andy Summers

PRINCE

Prince Rogers Nelson was born in Minneapolis on 7 June 1958. At the age of ten, he was taken to see the legendary soul performer, James Brown. Prince was inspired by the experience. Already an accomplished musician, he began furiously writing songs, and developing his technical expertise on bass, saxophone, guitar and drums.

GETTING STARTED

By the time he was 16, Prince was leading his third band, Flyte Time. Producer Chris Moon took a gamble, and allowed Prince free use of his studio during 'dead' time. The young musician produced a stunning demo tape and was snapped up by Warner Brothers to produce and record three albums. Prince was just 19. For his debut album, he insisted on doing everything himself. He racked up huge studio bills and went six times over budget. Sales of his debut were modest, but Warner kept faith. Prince

Prince's trademark was suggestive performances with his beloved guitar.

put a 'proper' band together for the next album, finished it in just six weeks – and hit the jackpot! 'Prince' went platinum, and one of its tracks, 'I Feel For You' gave Chaka Khan a No. 1 in 1984.

WHAT'S IN A NAME?

In 1993 Prince changed his name to the symbol that had first appeared a year earlier on the 'Love Symbol Album'. He insisted that all references to him should only display what unkindly became known as the 'squiggle'. Later, he insisted on being referred to as the 'Artist Formerly Known As Prince'. In '95, during his visit to the UK to receive a Brit Award, he refused to speak to the press and appeared at the ceremony with 'SLAVE' written across his face to draw attention to his bitter battle with Warner Brothers over their refusal to release 'Gold Experience'.

Prince in concert in March 1995.

ROYAL PERFORMER

By the '80s, Prince was a superstar. He toured the world with his extravagant show, featuring exotic dancers and of course, his own larger-than-life self.

His third album, 'Dirty Mind', was another solo effort. As its title suggests, it was sexually explicit – but there was more to it than just shock value. Critics agreed that it was a musical masterpiece. Two more albums quickly followed. 'Controversy' continued the funk style and sex content of its predecessor; '1999' revealed a new synthesiser-based sound.

MIXMASTER MUSICIAN

Prince's next project showed once and for all his ability to fuse different styles and come up with something refreshingly original. 'Purple Rain' was the soundtrack album to his semi-autobiographical movie. Its three singles, 'When Doves Cry', 'Let's Go Crazy' and 'Purple Rain', sold in their millions and the album itself earned Prince four Grammy Awards and an Oscar. In 1989, Prince gained his third US No. 1 with his soundtrack to the hit movie 'Batman'.

Leather-clad Prince stars in the award-winning film, 'Purple Rain'.

TOWARDS 1999

As the 1990s dawned, Prince's song 'Nothing Compares 2 U' topped the UK and US charts, performed by Irish singer Sinead O'Connor. In 1991, Prince assembled a brand new band, the New Power Generation. Their first album, 'Diamonds And Pearls', skilfully combined hip-hop and soul. Their second album together, 'Love Symbol Album', was a return to Prince's early form. Its raunchy single, 'Sexy MF', was banned from UK radio because of its suggestive lyrics! Prince has kept up his reputation as one of the most creative and controversial performers of recent years.

'Prince'
October '79
'Dirty Mind'
October '80
'1999'
February '83
'Purple Rain'
July '84

'Sign O' The Times'
March '87
'Love Symbol Album'
October '92
'The Hits: Volume I & II'
September '93

QUEEN

In 1959, Frederick Bulsara, aged 13, moved to London from his birthplace in Zanzibar. In 1973, Bulsara put out his first single, 'I Can Hear Music', calling himself Larry Lurex. But by then, he was already Queen's frontman under a different stage name – Freddie Mercury. *That* was the name that would make him famous.

SMILE, PLEASE!

In 1971 Mecury had started work with guitarist Brian May and drummer Roger Taylor in a band called Smile. They were soon joined by bassist John Deacon, and Queen were born. Their first single, 'Keep Yourself Alive', was released in July 1973, followed by a superb album debut, 'Queen'. There was no time for playing around as Larry Lurex!

The band toured the UK and USA with huge success in 1974. Their second album, 'Queen II' made the UK and US charts. Mercury's increasingly over-the-top leadership style and camp, glam-rock image were cheerfully indulged by the rest of the band. Queen remained tight-knit during their 18-year career – a rare feat in the ego-driven music business.

The king of camp: Mercury gave dazzling performances.

'Queen'
September '73
'Queen II'
April '74
'A Night At The Opera'
December '75
'Jazz'
November '78

'The Game'
July '80
'Hot Space'
May '82
'A Kind Of Magic'
June '86

WE ARE THE CHAMPIONS

In 1975 Queen released 'Bohemian Rhapsody'. The single stayed at No. 1 in the UK for nine weeks even though (or perhaps because) it broke all the rules of what a pop song was supposed to be. At six minutes long, it was twice the usual length for a single.

Its style was mock-opera and it was promoted by one of the first-ever music videos. Queen became international stars with a string of hits. Everyone knew at least some of the words to 'Killer Queen' or 'Bicycle Race'.

STADIUM ROCK

In 1980 Queen achieved their first US No. 1 single with the infectious 'Crazy Little Thing Called Love' and punchy 'Another One Bites The Dust', both taken from their No. 1 album, 'The Game'. They became used to performing to massive audiences. Of all the star-studded acts that took part in Live Aid, Queen slickly stole the show. Their aptly-named double album 'Live Magic' ('86) recorded Queen in their element – playing to massive crowds.

AIDS PANIC

One of the tragedies of the decade was the discovery of a 'new' disease, AIDS (Acquired Immune Deficiency Syndrome). The disease was not a killer in itself, but it destroyed the immune system, making its carrier unable to fight off even a simple cold. At first, no one knew how it was transmitted but it seemed to affect only homosexuals and the tabloids spread panic with stories of the 'gay plague'. In fact, the disease could affect anyone who had come into contact with HIV (Human Immuno-deficiency Virus), which was transmitted through sexual contact or through contact with infected blood.

But the 'plague' mentality of the early days lived on. Gay men and drug-users who shared needles had been at highest risk. Admitting that you had AIDS often revealed aspects of your lifestyle that had previously been private. Many sufferers, like Freddie Mercury, chose to keep their illness secret.

THE FINAL CURTAIN

By the start of the 1990s, Queen toured less and less. The press speculated on Mercury's health, but it was not until two days before his death that he announced he had AIDS. He became a victim of the ignorance of the risks of his decadent lifestyle. Mercury died on 24 November 1991. May, Taylor and Deacon held a memorial concert for him the next spring. Watched by over a billion people across the world, guest artists such as Elton John, George Michael, David Bowie and Annie Lennox paid tribute to one of rock's glitziest, best-loved superstars.

BRUCE SPRINGSTEEN

In 1974, the influential 'Rolling Stone' magazine critic Jon Landau bravely pronounced: "I've seen the future of rock 'n' roll – and its name is Bruce Springsteen!" Well, it was quite a prediction to live up to.

HUMBLE BEGINNINGS

Bruce Springsteen was born in Freehold, New Jersey on 23 September 1949. His father was variously a bus-driver and factory labourer and Springsteen experienced first-hand the social injustices which so many 'blue collar' Americans were experiencing. Throughout his entire career, he has never forgotten his working-class roots.

Springsteen got his first guitar when he was nine years old. By the time he left school, he had already written dozens of songs. In the mid- to late-'60s, he played in several local rock bands.

GOODBYE NEW JERSEY

Springsteen moved to Greenwich Village and in September 1971 formed the Bruce Springsteen Band.

Springsteen wears a rocker's bandanna.

Musicians came and went, but significant players were saxophonist Clarence Clemons and keyboard player David Sancious. In May 1972, Springsteen signed a deal with CBS to record ten albums over the next five years. The record label hoped to have signed the new Bob Dylan. Like Dylan's, Springsteen's songs used powerful, poetic lyrics to address complex issues. The first album was called 'Greetings From Asbury Park New Jersey'.

'Born To Run'
October '75
'The River'
October '80
'Nebraska'
September '82
'Born In The USA'
June '84

'Live 1975–1985'
December '86
'Tunnel Of Love'
October '87
'Greatest Hits'
February '95

It did not sell well. Neither did its follow-up, 'The Wild, The Innocent And The E Street Shuffle'. Nevertheless, Springsteen's reputation as a serious performer was growing. His next album, the explosive 'Born To Run', brought superstardom and a place in the US Top 5. Springsteen even appeared on the covers of 'Time' and 'Newsweek'.

BORN TO ROCK

The beginning of the 1980s saw the release of yet another masterpiece, 'The River'. Three tracks from the album were hit singles. In 1982, Springsteen bravely recorded 'Nebraska', a dark, moody and completely solo acoustic set.

HIT MAN

Two years later came his most accomplished album, 'Born In The USA'. The songs captured the angry mood of the poor and disadvantaged and turned it into belting rock. 'Born To Run' spent two years on the US and UK charts and gave him seven hit singles.

In 1986 Springsteen was voted the 'Best International Solo Artist' at the Brit Awards.

A FRESH START

In October 1987 Springsteen released the subdued 'Tunnel Of Love'. The dark mood reflected the state of his personal life. His two-and-a-half-year-old marriage was breaking up. But in 1990, Springsteen's new partner (and fellow-band member) Patti Scialfa announced she was pregnant. It was a bright start to another successful decade for the poor boy from the wrong side of the tracks!

"I've seen the future of rock 'n' roll..."

BRUCE THE BRAVE

Springsteen doesn't just write about social injustice. He raises funds for good causes in the way he knows best. He donated a live recording of 'Trapped' to the 'USA For Africa' album. He has also helped out Artists United Against Apartheid, the Harry Chapin Memorial Fund and the Human Rights Now Amnesty Tour. In 1990 he played a concert for Sting's Rainforest Conservation charity and also performed at a protest concert against alleged US government arms deals. A man true to his convictions!

Springsteen teamed up with singer-songwriter Paul Simon for the Harry Chapin Memorial Concert in aid of homeless kids.

TINA TURNER

Tina Turner's long career as a powerful singer has had two distinct and quite different phases. Annie Mae Bullock was born on the 26 November 1939 in Brownsville, Tennessee. As a teenager, her soulful voice was soon earning her a living in the smoky clubs around St Louis.

DOUBLE ACT

Tina was discovered by the established band leader Ike Turner. The pair married in 1958 and toured the USA with their successful rhythm and blues (R&B) act. With the gospel-inspired soul classic 'River Deep, Mountain High' ('66), they broke into the mainstream – in Europe, at least. With 'Proud Mary' ('71) and 'Nutbush City Limits' ('73), they became stars in the USA too.

Tina was the star of the show, and her possessive husband found this hard to handle. In 1975, Tina, no longer in awe of Ike's bullying both on- and off-stage, walked out of the stormy marriage. She was free at last. She gave a sizzling performance as the Acid Queen in the Who's film musical, 'Tommy'. But then came a lean period – until the 1980s.

A FRESH START

Tina Turner had always had a big UK following. UK synth-pop band Heaven 17 invited her to work with them in 1983, and she eagerly agreed. This led to a new contract with Capitol Records. Tina was 45 years old. Out came a husky cover of an Al Green song.

Ike and Tina's duo lasted for 17 years.

'Let's Stay Together' made the Top 20 on both sides of the Atlantic. In 1984, Tina recorded her comeback album 'Private Dancer'. Its tormented title track (about a lonely stripper) was written by Mark Knopfler; the album also featured the No. 1 single, 'What's Love Got To Do With It'. Tina especially appealed to 40-somethings who had heard her singing first time around. They were delighted to discover she was still just as sexy and energetic 20 years on.

Turner wowed film-goers with her role in 'Mad Max'.

SHOW-STOPPER

In 1984 Tina astutely accepted a part in the sci-fi adventure movie 'Mad Max: Beyond The Thunderdome'. The theme song, 'We Don't Need Another Hero', was delivered with her trademark gutsy passion and gave her another massive hit. Tina concentrated on projecting her stage persona as a wild, larger-than-life soul and rock performer. Over 180,000 came to her show in Rio de Janeiro and she performed to millions at Live Aid.

GLAMOROUS GRANNY

In 1993 Tina's autobiography was filmed as 'What's Love Got To Do With It?'. Soon after, Tina decided to spend more time with her family (which includes her grandchildren!) and to develop her interest in Buddhism.

However, the superstar couldn't resist doing the title song for a Bond film, 'Golden Eye', in 1995 and the following year she was back in the studio to record 'Wildest Dreams' with producer Trevor Horn.

'Acid Queen'
October '75
'Private Dancer'
June '84
'Break Every Rule'
September '86

'Proud Mary & Other Hits' (with Ike Turner)
December '88
'Foreign Affair'
September '89
'Simply The Best'
October '91

CHARITY ROCK

In 1984 the world was shocked by footage of the Ethiopian famine. Ex-Boomtown Rat Bob Geldof decided to do something about it. Together with Midge Ure, he wrote the charity single 'Do They Know It's Christmas?'.

The following summer Live Aid, performed live from London and Philadelphia, raised more for the cause. The galaxy of stars included Tina Turner who sang 'Honky Tonk Woman' with Mick Jagger.

Broadcast live around the world, the concert raised over £50 million.

U2

Musicians Paul Hewson, David Evans, Adam Clayton and Larry Mullen Jr. started playing covers in Dublin's pubs and youth clubs in 1977. Known as Feedback (and later, Hype), they played Beach Boys', Stones' and Shadows' songs for a pittance, until their above-average musical prowess won them a talent contest staged in Limerick in 1978. Hewson became Bono, Evans re-named himself the Edge – and, most importantly, Hype became U2.

U2: THE EARLY YEARS

Astute local manager Paul McGuiness spotted their potential, and secured a recording contract with CBS. Their first two releases topped the Irish charts, and U2 were keen to repeat their success outside their native land. They started their first album with producer Steve Lillywhite. 'Boy' (1980) dealt sensitively with the pangs and problems of adolescence, and was warmly praised by the critics.

U2 were gaining a well deserved reputation as a

performing band, thanks to Bono's raw singing power and the rock-solid backing of his musical colleagues.

They toured America in 1981, and then released their second album, 'October'. They were at last finding their true voice. This moving set was followed by a single called, 'New Year's Day'.

Frontman Bono delivers another belter.

Written in support of the Polish Solidarity movement, it entered the Top 10 in January 1983. A month later, their new album, 'War', topped the UK charts. Fiercely political in content, 'War' opened with the blistering 'Sunday, Bloody Sunday'. The song referred back to January '72, when the British Army opened fire on Catholic protestors and killed 14 people.

'October'
October '81
'War'
February '83
'The Unforgettable Fire'
October '84

'The Joshua Tree'
March '87
'Rattle & Hum'
October '88
'Achtung Baby'
November '91

MUSIC WITH A MESSAGE

U2's next release, the EP 'Under A Blood Red Sky' (1983), documented their impressive stage show. But their political conscience was not neglected. 'The Unforgettable Fire' included their tribute to the black civil rights leader Martin Luther King Jr., 'Pride (In The Name of Love)'. Next came the outstanding 'The Joshua Tree', another chart-topping hit.

WE ARE THE PASSENGERS

After a couple of quiet years, U2 returned in 1991 with a new sound. Their inspired album 'Achtung Baby', produced by Brian Eno, drew heavily on dance music and techno. Hailed as their best album yet, it went straight to No. 1!

In 1995 they collaborated on Eno's 'Passengers' project, along with opera star Luciano Pavarotti. Another good cause – this time for the children of Bosnia. In the late 1990s, U2 maintain their reputation as one of the world's most exciting bands. But quite clearly, their huge success has not gone to their heads.

IRISH MUSIC

For centuries Irish Protestants and Catholics have been unable to bury completely their religious differences. Irish people have suffered immense poverty, oppression and deprivation and their artists have chosen to express their anguish in the way they know best.

U2's Irish background was the perfect education for producing music with a message.

Traditional Gaelic music ranges from swirling poetic ballads to furious jigs and reels played on a variety of acoustic instruments – such as guitars, banjos, mandolins, fiddles, whistles – to appreciative audiences in pubs and clubs.

Music-making is informal at a 'ceili'.

U2 in their video, 'Rattle & Hum'.

WHAM!

When Yorgos Kyriako Panayiotou befriended schoolmate Andrew Ridgeley at Bushey Meads Comprehensive school in the mid-'70s, the pair quickly discovered their mutual interest in soul, reggae, dance and ska music. They decided that music would be their passport to fame. Yorgos rechristened himself George Michael, and he and Andrew formed a ska band, the Executive.

WHAM!
'Fantastic'
July '83
'Make It Big'
November '84

GEORGE MICHAEL
'Faith'
November '87
'Listen Without Prejudice Volume One'
August '90

WHAM! BAM!

In 1982 they formed their own duo, Wham!, and spent hours composing and recording Michael's songs, then sending demos of their work to every record company they could think of. Their persistence paid off. Small local record company Innervision gave them an advance of £500 and the freedom to write, record and produce their first single. Out came 'Wham! Rap (Enjoy What You Do)' with the boys backed by singers Amanda Washbourn and Shirlie Holliman. The record attracted little attention. However, their second single for Innervision brought them overnight success. 'Young Guns (Go For It)' went to No. 3 in the UK charts and projected an image of leatherclad rebels. Less than a year later, Wham!'s third single, 'Bad Boys' was equally successful. Their first album, 'Fantastic', was a fantastic success and went straight to No. 1! The pair had hordes of teenage fans, thanks to the macho image portrayed in their stylish videos and slick stage show.

Wham! make their debut with 'Wham! Rap (Enjoy What You Do)'.

AMERICAN DREAM

'Club Tropicana' and 'Club Fantastic Megamix' provided Wham! with two more Top 10 hits, but the boys were eager to make it big in the USA, where the real money was to be made. Record giant Columbia had noticed Michael's songwriting skills and the band's punchy videos.

Wham! hit the No. 1 spot with 'Wake Me Up Before You Go-Go' in May 1984. Their next single, 'Careless Whisper', was a much slower ballad – but nevertheless a hit.

In the same year 'Freedom' and their aptly-titled album, 'Make It Big', hit the jackpot again. Suddenly Wham! were one of the hottest acts in the world.

Wham!'s Christmas single that year, titled 'Last Christmas', was only prevented from making the No. 1 spot by

The handsome stars were idolised by their teenage fans.

the charity number from Band Aid (to which they had contributed). Nevertheless 'Last Christmas' sold more copies in the UK than any other Wham! or George Michael single before or since.

THE END

March 1986 saw a significant release: 'A Different Corner' that was credited to Michael alone. The pair went their separate ways. George Michael's first official solo album, 'Faith' proved he could repeat Wham!'s success on his own. In 1990 he appealed to his audience to 'Listen Without Prejudice'. They did, and provided him with his fifth No. 1 album!

GOODBYE BOYS!

Nobody could deny that in terms of creativity, George Michael was the driving force of Wham! He wrote the songs and played most of the instruments on the recordings. Certainly, Andrew Ridgeley's post-Wham! career has been less than startling. His 1990 album 'Son Of Albert' didn't even make the US Top 100.

However, at least the boys went out with a bang. Their final concert in London's Wembley Stadium was attended by over 80,000 fans!

Wham! sing farewell to their fans on-stage at Wembley, July 1986.

GAZETTEER

The 1980s was a rich decade for music and the previous chapters have included only a few of its stars. The audience for pop was bigger than ever and new styles sprang up to suit every taste.

INXS

BIG SOUNDS

Australian band INXS filled stadiums around the world and moved smoothly between rock 'n' roll, pop and dancey beats. The decade also saw old-timers Status Quo still going strong, although they had to wait until the '90s for the second No. 1 of their long career with their football anthem 'Come On You Reds'.

GOING SOLO

There were lots of talented solo stars to enjoy. Kate Bush dazzled with songs such as 'Running Up That Hill'. She also worked with Peter Gabriel, who had left Genesis in 1975. Gabriel had hits in the '80s with 'Sledgehammer' and 'Big Time'. His replacement as Genesis's frontman, Phil Collins, also launched a solo career. He won a Grammy for his album 'No Jacket Required' ('85). Nigerian singer Sade cornered the pop-meets-jazz market with her stunning debut 'Diamond Life' in '84 – another Grammy-winner. And Jamaican diva Grace Jones had a hit with the extraordinary 'Slave To The Rhythm' in '85.

Phil Collins

MUSIC MACHINES

Computers began to play an important role. Spandau Ballet, Human League, Simple Minds, Depeche Mode and Tears For Fears were just some of the bands which moved away from traditional instruments. They experimented with synthesisers, drum machines and new recording techniques to produce highly original 'synth pop'. Producer Trevor Horn took electronica a step further with his outfit the Art of Noise. No 'band' featured on the video of their hit 'Close (To the Edit)', which was made up of samples of other tracks chopped up and stitched back together.

Grace Jones

IN THE MIX

Samplers and drum machines were central in creating a new musical form – 'house music'. Named after the acid house parties where it was played, this music featured unfeasibly fast beats and squelchy electronic sounds.

Spandau Ballet

Human League

IT'S A RAP!

Rap and hip-hop were born. Taking inspiration from the fast-talking reggae 'toasters', rappers spoke their fiercely political lyrics. Rap expressed the 'gangsta' culture of young African-Americans. Pioneers of the sound included Run DMC (the first rap stars to appear on MTV), Grandmaster Flash and Ice-T.

Run DMC

PUBLICITY MACHINE

Performers such as the Smiths, Style Council and Billy Bragg all used their music to publicly express their strong political beliefs. And of course, popular music wouldn't be complete without its show-offs. Frankie Goes To Hollywood were hugely hyped. Their controversial debut single 'Relax' was banned by the BBC. Culture Club first topped the charts with 'Do You Really Want To Hurt Me', sung by glamorous Boy George whose gender-bending image attracted lots of press attention!

Frankie Goes To Hollywood

Culture Club

INDEX

PHOTOGRAPHIC CREDITS *Abbreviations: t-top, m-middle, b-bottom, r-right, l-left, c-centre. Front cover all, 3, 6 both, 9b, 10t, 12t, 14t & bl, 15l, 16b, 16-17, 17b, 18t & m, 23r, 24m, 26t, 26-27, 31m & br - E. Roberts/Redferns. 4-5, 12-13, 13b, 22m & b - R. Aaron/Redferns. 7t - Warner/Goldcrest (courtesy Kobal). 7m, 8b, 10b, 20t, 24t & 31tl - D. Redfern/Redferns. 7b - H. Baum/Redferns. 8t - T. Hall/Redferns. 8c & 20 - Suzi Gibbons/Redferns. 9t - Mark Young/Redferns. 10t - G. Davis/Redferns. 11t & 18-19 - Frank Spooner Pictures. 11b - Rex Features. 12t - G. Baker/Redferns. 13t - Stigwood/Hemdale (courtesy Kobal). 14br - Cinergi Pictures (courtesy Kobal). 17t - S. Cunningham. 18b - K. Doherty. 19 & 25t - Warner Bros (courtesy Kobal). 20t, 28b, 29t & 30m - I. Dickenson/Redferns. 22t & 30t - B. King/Redferns. 23l - A. Putler/Redferns. 24b - T. Hanley/Redferns. 25b - M. Cameron/Redferns. 26b - C. Zlotnik/Redferns. 27b - Paramount (courtesy Kobal). 28t - S. & G/Redferns. 29m & b - M. Hutson/Redferns. 31m & bl - NE/Redferns.*